Friendship Bracelets: Ho

Beautiful Bracelets for B

Step-by-Step Guide to Making Colorful
Patterns, Creative Knots, and Meaningful DIY
Friendship Gifts for All Skill Levels

Bernice Thadeus

Table of Content

Chapter 1

Getting Started

Before diving into your first friendship bracelet, let's take a moment to appreciate how wonderfully simple and rewarding this craft truly is. You don't need a large studio, complicated tools, or expensive supplies. All you need are a few essential materials, a small space to work comfortably, and most importantly, a creative heart that's ready to play with colors, patterns, and textures.

The beauty of friendship bracelet making lies in its accessibility — it welcomes everyone. Whether you're a student making bracelets during study breaks, a parent looking for a relaxing pastime, or a seasoned crafter searching for a portable creative hobby, this art form meets you exactly where you are.

In this chapter, we'll explore the fundamental tools and materials you'll need and how to set up a cozy, efficient workspace. Think of this as your personal foundation — once you have the right setup, you can focus entirely on creativity and flow.

Essential Tools and Materials

Embroidery Floss (Cotton Thread)

Embroidery floss is the star of the show. This smooth, slightly glossy, and colorful thread is traditionally used in embroidery, but it's also the classic choice for friendship bracelet making. Each skein of embroidery floss usually contains six fine strands twisted together — you can use them as they are or separate them for finer designs.

When you're just starting out, choose medium-weight cotton embroidery floss, as it's easier to handle and gives your knots an even, tidy look. Thin threads can tangle easily, while thick cords can feel bulky and stiff.

Experiment with color combinations that speak to you — bright, bold hues for playful bracelets, or soft pastels for delicate, elegant designs. Some crafters love to use gradient or variegated threads, which change color gradually along their length, giving a beautiful ombré effect.

Pro Tip: Always buy extra thread in your favorite shades. It's surprising how quickly you'll fall in love with the process and want to make more!

Scissors

A sharp pair of scissors may not sound exciting, but it's one of the most important tools you'll use. Dull scissors can fray the ends of your thread, making knotting more difficult and leaving messy edges. Invest in a small pair of precision craft scissors or embroidery scissors — they give you more control and cleaner cuts.

Keep your scissors dedicated to thread cutting only; using them on paper or fabric dulls the blades over time. If you plan to travel with your bracelet-making kit, look for scissors with a protective cap or folding design.

Pro Tip: If you're working on-the-go, a small thread cutter pendant or craft knife can serve as a compact and safe alternative.

Tape, Clipboard, or Safety Pin

You'll need a way to secure your bracelet while you work — otherwise, it will twist, slip, or unravel before your masterpiece even begins.

Here are three simple and effective options:

Tape: Perfect for working on a flat surface like a table, desk, or countertop. Choose a strong tape (like masking or painter's tape) that holds firmly without damaging your surface or threads.

Clipboard: A favorite among crafters! It's portable, keeps your work in place, and can be used anywhere — even on your lap while watching TV or sitting in the park. Simply clip the loop or starting knot at the top, and your bracelet will stay taut while you knot away.

Safety Pin: Ideal if you like working from the comfort of your couch or bed. Pin your bracelet's loop or knot to a cushion, pillow, or even your jeans, and your work will stay securely anchored as you weave.

Pro Tip: Try each method to see what feels most natural. Some crafters even use a combination — a clipboard for home projects and a safety pin for travel or outdoor crafting.

Measuring Tape or Ruler

Accurate measurements make your bracelets consistent and comfortable to wear. A measuring tape or ruler helps ensure you cut your threads long enough — generally 30–40 inches (75–100 cm) per strand.

It's better to err on the side of caution and cut slightly longer threads, as you can always trim excess later. The length you need will depend on your pattern, knot density, and wrist size, but as a rule of thumb:

4–6 strands: 30 inches each (simple patterns)

8–12 strands: 36–40 inches each (complex designs)

Pro Tip: If you're making a bracelet for someone else, measure their wrist and add about 4–6 inches to account for knots and loops.

Optional Additions for Creative Flair

Once you get comfortable with the basics, you may want to elevate your designs with a touch of personality and style. Here are some optional — but delightful — extras to keep on hand:

Beads or Charms: Add sparkle, texture, or symbolism to your bracelets. Choose lightweight beads that fit snugly on your threads. Letter beads are perfect for spelling names or meaningful words.

Needle: A fine needle helps thread beads onto embroidery floss, especially if the bead holes are small.

Fabric Glue or Clear Nail Polish: Use a dab to seal your knots or prevent fraying at the ends. Both options dry clear and add durability without altering the bracelet's appearance.

Pro Tip: Store small beads or charms in mini containers or resealable bags. It keeps your workspace tidy and prevents the dreaded bead spill!

Setting Up Your Workspace

Your workspace doesn't have to be elaborate — even a small corner of your kitchen table, a coffee table, or a desk will do. What matters most is comfort, good lighting, and organization.

Choose the Right Space

Find a spot where you can relax without distractions. Good lighting is essential — natural daylight is best, but a soft desk lamp will also do wonders, especially during evening crafting sessions.

Organize Your Materials

Use small storage boxes, jars, or even recycled containers to sort your embroidery floss by color. You can wind each skein onto a small piece of cardboard or plastic bobbin to prevent tangling. Keeping your threads visible and organized not only saves time but also sparks creativity as you see all the color combinations at once.

A simple organizer tray can hold your scissors, safety pins, and tape, while a small pouch or container makes it easy to take your bracelet-making kit wherever inspiration strikes — whether you're at home, on a road trip, or relaxing outdoors.

Comfort and Posture

Bracelet making involves repetitive hand movements, so it's important to sit comfortably. Choose a chair that supports your back, and keep your elbows slightly bent as you knot. Take short breaks to stretch your fingers and wrists — this prevents stiffness and helps maintain precision in your knots.

Create a Calming Atmosphere

Friendship bracelet making is not just about crafting; it's a meditative and joyful experience. Set the mood by playing gentle music, lighting a candle, or simply working in a quiet environment. Many crafters find that making bracelets is a form of mindfulness — each knot encourages patience, presence, and creativity.

Grab a cup of tea or coffee, settle into your space, and enjoy the rhythm of knotting. The more relaxed and focused you feel, the more even and beautiful your bracelets will turn out.

Final Thoughts Before You Begin

Setting up your tools and workspace might seem like a small step, but it lays the foundation for an enjoyable and successful crafting experience. Think of this chapter as the beginning of your creative ritual — a moment to slow down, prepare your space, and get in touch with your artistic side.

With your materials ready and your space organized, you're all set to embark on your first bracelet project. In the next chapter, we'll dive into the fascinating world of knots — the building blocks of every friendship bracelet. You'll learn how to hold your threads, make your first knots, and start creating patterns that reflect your unique style.

Take a deep breath, smile, and get ready to create something beautiful — because the journey from simple threads to heartfelt bracelets starts right here, with you.

Chapter 2

Understanding Friendship Bracelet Basics

Before we begin tying knots and crafting your first bracelet, it's important to pause and understand the foundation of this beautiful art form. Every craft, no matter how simple it appears, has a story and a rhythm — a set of basic principles that transform ordinary materials into something meaningful. Friendship bracelets are no exception.

In this chapter, we'll explore the fascinating history behind friendship bracelets, uncover the deeper symbolism they carry, and learn about the language of knots — the essential building blocks that give every bracelet its strength, beauty, and soul.

By the end of this chapter, you'll not only know how friendship bracelets are made but why they hold such lasting charm across generations and cultures.

A Brief History of Friendship Bracelets

Friendship bracelets may look like a modern craft trend, but their roots run deep — stretching back centuries and crossing continents. The exact origin is difficult to trace, but the most well-documented beginnings point to Central and South America, particularly among the Indigenous peoples of Guatemala, Mexico, and parts of the Andes.

These early bracelets were often woven from natural fibers like cotton or hemp and dyed with vibrant plant-based pigments. Each bracelet was more than just an ornament — it was a symbol of unity, peace, and connection among tribes and communities. Colors, patterns, and knots often carried specific meanings — a silent language of emotion and intention.

The Tradition of Tying and Wishing

The practice of exchanging friendship bracelets as tokens of affection and loyalty became popular through cultural exchange in the late 20th century. In many traditions, the giver ties the bracelet onto the wrist of a friend or loved one while the receiver silently makes a wish. The bracelet is worn continuously until it naturally falls off, at which point the wish is believed to come true.

This ritual, while simple, captures something profound — the beauty of impermanence. A friendship bracelet, like life and love itself, is temporary in form but lasting in meaning. The fading colors, frayed ends, and eventual unraveling symbolize growth, transformation, and the ever-evolving nature of human connection.

The Global Spread of a Craft of Connection

By the 1970s and 1980s, friendship bracelets found new life through the peace and hippie movements, where they became symbols of love, unity, and anti-materialism. People began making them not just for friends but as emblems of equality and shared humanity. From handmade markets to summer camps and schoolyards, friendship bracelet making became a universal expression of creativity and care.

Today, friendship bracelets are crafted worldwide — not just by children or hobbyists, but also by artists, designers, and entrepreneurs who have elevated them into wearable art. Despite evolving designs and materials, one thing remains unchanged: every friendship bracelet is still a handmade symbol of thoughtfulness.

When you make one, you're continuing a tradition that's been passed down through generations — a small but powerful act of connection.

The Language of Knots

Now that you understand the cultural and emotional roots of friendship bracelets, let's move on to the technical foundation: knots.

Every friendship bracelet, no matter how simple or intricate, is built entirely from a series of knots. Think of knots as the alphabet of this craft — once you learn the four basic types, you can combine them in endless ways to form patterns, letters, shapes, and color gradients.

Learning to tie knots may seem repetitive at first, but it's actually meditative. Each knot carries rhythm and intention. The gentle pulling and tightening can be incredibly soothing — a mindful process that connects your hands, heart, and focus.

Understanding the Four Basic Knots

There are four essential knots that form the foundation of every friendship bracelet pattern:

Forward Knot (FK) – moves thread from left to right.

Backward Knot (BK) – moves thread from right to left.

Forward-Backward Knot (FBK) – used to switch directions from left to right and back again.

Backward-Forward Knot (BFK) – used to switch directions from right to left and back again.

Let's take a closer look at each one, step by step.

1. The Forward Knot (FK)

The forward knot is the most common and fundamental knot in bracelet making. It creates diagonal lines that slant to the right — perfect for simple patterns like the classic candy stripe.

How to Make a Forward Knot:

Hold your base (stationary) thread in your left hand and your working thread in your right hand.

Cross the working thread over the base thread, forming the shape of the number "4."

Bring the end of the working thread under the base thread and pull it through the loop you just made.

Pull the knot gently upward to tighten it near the top.

Repeat once more — remember, every full knot is made of two half-knots.

The motion feels like drawing a "4" shape with your thread. Keep your tension consistent — not too tight (which can cause curling) and not too loose (which makes gaps).

The forward knot "pushes" color and direction from left to right, creating clean, angled lines that build beautiful, rhythmic designs.

2. The Backward Knot (BK)

The backward knot is essentially the mirror image of the forward knot. Instead of slanting right, it slants left, moving your working thread from right to left.

How to Make a Backward Knot:

Hold your base thread in your right hand and your working thread in your left.

Cross the working thread over the base thread, forming a backward "4" shape.

Bring the end under the base thread and through the loop.

Pull it up and tighten gently near the top.

Repeat once more to complete a full knot.

This knot is crucial for creating symmetrical patterns like chevrons or diamonds, where the left and right sides mirror each other.

Pro Tip:

If you're right-handed, backward knots may feel less natural at first. Practice slowly, focusing on the movement. Soon your hands will remember the rhythm.

3. The Forward-Backward Knot (FBK)

This knot is your key to direction changes. It starts as a forward knot but ends as a backward one. It keeps your working thread on the same side rather than moving it across.

How to Make a Forward-Backward Knot:

Begin by tying the first half as a forward knot ("4" shape, pull upward).

Instead of tying another forward half, switch directions and tie the second half as a backward knot (a backward "4").

The FBK is especially useful when your pattern needs one color to continue downward on the same side, or when you're outlining shapes in two-tone designs.

4. The Backward-Forward Knot (BFK)

Like the FBK, this knot helps you switch direction — but it starts backward and ends forward.

How to Make a Backward-Forward Knot:

Begin with a backward "4" and tie the first half-knot.

Then switch direction and tie the second half as a forward knot ("4" shape).

This knot allows your working thread to remain in place without traveling to the opposite side, which is essential for patterns that require mirroring or balancing.

The Secret to Perfect Knots — Tension and Consistency

The difference between a messy bracelet and a neat, professional-looking one often comes down to a single factor: tension consistency.

When you pull too tightly, your bracelet can twist or curl. Too loosely, and the knots will look uneven and floppy. The key is to find a comfortable rhythm — firm but gentle, secure but flexible.

Imagine the thread as a living material — it responds best when treated with patience and care. As you practice, you'll develop muscle memory and instinctively adjust your tension for even rows.

Try This Exercise:

Cut two short threads and practice tying rows of forward knots. Focus on how your hands move and how each knot feels. Soon, your fingers will learn the natural pull required for balanced, even work.

Holding the Threads — The Art of Control

How you hold your threads matters just as much as how you tie them. Keep your base thread taut but not stretched, and use your dominant hand to control the working thread.

Some crafters prefer to anchor their base threads under their thumb, while others like to secure them with a pin or clip. Experiment until you find your most comfortable technique. Remember — you're not just tying knots; you're dancing with the thread. The smoother the movement, the more graceful your results.

Practice Makes Patterns

Once you've learned the four basic knots, you hold the key to an infinite world of designs. Every pattern — from simple stripes to intricate hearts or zigzags — is built from these same knots, just arranged in different sequences and directions.

Think of it like learning to write: once you know the letters, you can form any word or sentence you like. With friendship bracelets, once you master the knots, your imagination is the only limit.

A Final Thought: The Meditation in Motion

Knot by knot, color by color, friendship bracelet making becomes more than a hobby

— it turns into a peaceful practice of mindfulness. The repetitive movements quiet the mind, the bright colors lift the spirit, and the final product carries meaning and love.

So as you begin practicing your knots, don't rush. Enjoy each pull, each loop, each tiny success. With every knot you tie, you're not just learning a skill — you're weaving patience, intention, and joy into something beautiful.

Chapter 3

Mastering the Basic Techniques

Now that you've learned about the origins of friendship bracelets and the language of knots, it's time to bring everything together with hands-on practice. This chapter is where your creative journey truly begins — where threads turn into art and patience transforms into beautiful patterns.

Before you dive into complex designs, it's essential to understand the basic techniques that will serve as your foundation. You'll learn how to cut and arrange your threads, how to tie forward and backward knots with confidence, and how to read patterns like a pro. These skills may seem simple at first, but they are the stepping stones toward creating any friendship bracelet you can imagine.

So take a deep breath, get comfortable, and prepare to let your fingers do the magic.

1. Cutting and Arranging Threads

The very first step in any friendship bracelet project is preparing your threads. The way you cut, fold, and arrange them sets the tone for how easy and enjoyable your crafting experience will be.

Choosing Your Colors

For your first bracelet, I recommend using 4 to 8 colors of embroidery floss. Using fewer colors will make it easier to see your pattern develop, while adding more will create complex, colorful results once you're comfortable with the basics.

Think about the color palette that makes you feel happy or inspired. Are you drawn to cool ocean tones like blue, green, and white? Or do you prefer warm sunset hues like orange, pink, and gold? Don't overthink it — choose what speaks to you. Color is personal and emotional, and it adds character to your work.

Pro Tip: Arrange your colors in a way that complements your design. Lighter shades can be balanced with darker ones for contrast, or you can use an ombré progression — from light to dark — for a soft gradient effect.

Measuring and Cutting the Threads

Cut each strand to a length of about 30–40 inches (75–100 cm). If you're unsure, always cut a little extra — you can trim the ends later, but you can't add more thread once you've started knotting.

For example:

Simple patterns: 4 strands at 30 inches each.

More complex patterns: 6–8 strands at 36–40 inches each.

Line up the ends neatly, making sure none are shorter than the others. Hold all strands together and fold them in half. At the folded end, tie an overhand knot about two inches down — this creates a loop, which will serve as the closure for your bracelet.

This loop is important because it not only helps you start your work neatly but also gives you a simple way to tie the finished bracelet around your wrist.

Securing Your Bracelet

Before you start knotting, you'll need to anchor your bracelet so it doesn't move around. There are several ways to do this:

Tape Method: Place a piece of masking or painter's tape over the loop and stick it firmly to a table or desk. This works well if you're crafting at a flat surface.

Clipboard Method: Place the loop under the metal clip of a clipboard. This is a favorite among crafters because it's portable and stable.

Safety Pin Method: Attach the loop to a soft surface such as a cushion, pillow, or even your jeans. This option is perfect for working in a relaxed, seated position.

Whichever method you choose, make sure the threads are taut but not stretched tight. You want a little give, as this will help you make even, comfortable knots.

Arranging Your Threads

Lay your strands flat, separating them so that the colors are arranged in your chosen order. The arrangement you choose here will directly affect the pattern of your bracelet. For example:

A rainbow order will produce colorful stripes.

A mirrored order (e.g., blue, pink, yellow, pink, blue) will produce symmetrical designs like chevrons or hearts.

Once your colors are set, smooth the threads with your fingers and make sure they're not tangled. Congratulations — you've just set the stage for your first bracelet!

2. Making Forward and Backward Knots

Now comes the exciting part — learning to tie the two most essential knots in friendship bracelet making: the Forward Knot (FK) and the Backward Knot (BK). Mastering these two movements will allow you to create nearly any design imaginable.

Remember that each full knot is made up of two half knots. This repetition ensures that your rows are even and your pattern stays consistent.

The Forward Knot (FK)

The forward knot moves from left to right and creates a diagonal slant in that direction.

It's used in many beginner patterns, such as the candy stripe bracelet.

Step-by-Step Guide:

Choose the leftmost thread as your working thread and the one next to it as your base thread.

Cross the working thread over the base thread to form the shape of the number "4."

Bring the end of the working thread under the base thread and up through the loop of the "4."

Gently pull the working thread upward to tighten the knot near the top. Don't yank too hard — just enough to make it snug.

Repeat the process once more. Two half knots make one complete forward knot.

You'll notice the working thread has now moved one position to the right. Continue making forward knots across the row, and you'll see neat diagonal lines forming as you go.

Pro Tip: Keep your knots uniform by holding the base thread steady while pulling upward with the working thread. Consistent tension is key to creating a professional finish.

The Backward Knot (BK)

The backward knot is the mirror image of the forward knot and moves from right to left. It's used to create left-slanting patterns and for balancing symmetrical designs like chevrons.

Step-by-Step Guide:

Choose the rightmost thread as your working thread and the one next to it on the left as your base thread.

Cross the working thread over the base thread to form a backward "4" shape.

Bring the end of the working thread under the base thread and up through the loop.

Pull it gently upward to tighten the first half-knot.

Repeat once more for the second half-knot to complete a full backward knot.

As you complete each knot, the working thread will move one position to the left. If you look closely, you'll see that your knots form diagonal ridges that lean in the opposite direction of the forward knot.

Practice Exercise: Building Confidence

Before diving into your first pattern, it's a good idea to practice these two knots separately.

Start with four strands in two colors — two for the left side and two for the right.

Use one color to practice forward knots across all the others. Then switch and practice backward knots in the opposite direction.

After a few rows, your hands will start to move more naturally. You'll feel the rhythm — a gentle pull, a steady beat — as the threads flow between your fingers.

Don't worry if your knots aren't perfect right away. Even the most experienced crafters started with uneven tension and crooked lines. Each bracelet you make will teach you something new.

3. Reading Patterns

Once you've mastered the mechanics of knotting, the next step is understanding how to read friendship bracelet patterns. Think of patterns as musical notation for your craft — they tell you when to move left or right, when to switch colors, and when to change directions.

A friendship bracelet pattern is typically represented as a grid made up of dots and arrows. Each arrow tells you which knot to make, and each column represents a thread in your bracelet.

Here's how to interpret them:

Arrows pointing right ($\rightarrow$) = Forward Knot (FK)

Arrows pointing left ($\leftarrow$) = Backward Knot (BK)

Arrows pointing right then left ($\leftrightarrow$) = Forward-Backward Knot (FBK)

Arrows pointing left then right ($\updownarrow$) = Backward-Forward Knot (BFK)

When you follow these arrows row by row, you're essentially tracing the path of your threads. Over time, you'll begin to recognize familiar sequences that create specific designs — like chevrons, diamonds, and stripes.

Pro Tip:

Start with simple patterns (4–6 strands) before progressing to complex ones. Print or draw your patterns on paper, and use a pencil to mark each row as you complete it. This helps you stay organized and prevents mistakes.

A Note on Patience and Practice

The techniques you've learned in this chapter form the backbone of every friendship bracelet you'll ever make. At first, your knots may feel clumsy or uneven — that's completely normal. With practice, your hands will begin to remember the rhythm, and the process will feel as natural as breathing.

As you practice, try to relax your shoulders and enjoy the repetition. Making friendship bracelets isn't just about creating something pretty — it's a form of creative meditation. Every knot is a tiny act of focus and care, and every row brings you closer to a finished piece filled with personality and intention.

Looking Ahead

In the next chapter, we'll move from practice to play. You'll learn how to combine these knots into recognizable stitches and beginner patterns, including stripes, chevrons, and simple geometric designs. With your tools ready and your knots mastered, you're about to see your first bracelet truly take shape — one colorful knot at a time.

So take a sip of tea, stretch your fingers, and prepare for the joy of turning thread into art.

Chapter 4

Beginner Stitches and Pattern Practice

Now that you've learned the language of knots and mastered the basic techniques, it's time to bring your skills to life with simple yet beautiful patterns. This is where you begin to see your efforts take shape — rows of colorful threads transforming into cheerful stripes, bold chevrons, and playful dotted textures.

Before tackling the full-length projects later in this book, we'll focus on four beginner-friendly stitch patterns that will strengthen your control, improve your rhythm, and build your confidence:

Candy Stripe Pattern – cheerful, classic diagonal stripes.

Chevron Pattern – balanced, symmetrical "V" shapes.

Diagonal Dots Pattern – a fun twist that adds texture.

Braided and Twisted Ties – finishing techniques for professional, tidy ends.

These foundational stitches are the "training ground" for your friendship bracelet journey. Once you feel comfortable with them, you'll be able to tackle any pattern, no matter how intricate.

Let's get started — knot by knot, row by row.

1. The Candy Stripe Pattern

If friendship bracelets had a signature look, it would be the candy stripe. Its neat diagonal lines, bright colors, and rhythmic flow make it the perfect beginner pattern. It's straightforward, meditative, and wonderfully satisfying to watch as the stripes grow longer with every knot.

What You'll Learn

Forward knots (FK)

Maintaining even tension

Understanding thread progression

Materials

4–6 colors of embroidery floss (30–40 inches each)

Tape, clipboard, or safety pin

Scissors

Setup

Cut your chosen threads to the same length and tie an overhand knot about 2 inches from the top to form your loop.

Secure your bracelet to your workspace.

Arrange your threads in the order you want your colors to appear in stripes — for example, red, yellow, green, blue.

How to Make the Pattern

Start with the leftmost thread (Color 1). This is your working thread.

Tie forward knots (two half-knots) over each of the threads to its right, one at a time.

Forward knot over Color 2 → Forward knot over Color 3 → Forward knot over Color 4, and so on.

Once you've tied all the way across, your working thread (Color 1) will end up on the far right.

Now, your next color (Color 2, which is now on the far left) becomes your new working thread.

Repeat the same process, tying forward knots across all remaining threads.

With each row, the diagonal stripes will start to appear, flowing gently from the upper left to the lower right.

Tips for Success

Consistency is key: Try to make each knot the same tightness.

Neatness over speed: Don't rush — it's better to have clean, even rows than fast, uneven ones.

Watch your color order: The thread you start with will always travel across to the far right.

Reflection

Once you finish a few inches, pause and look at your work. You'll notice that every stripe represents your growing confidence and patience. This pattern teaches rhythm, flow, and discipline — the true spirit of bracelet making.

2. The Chevron Pattern

If the candy stripe is your introduction to flow, the chevron pattern teaches you harmony. The chevron, with its striking "V"

shape, is one of the most beloved designs in friendship bracelet making. It symbolizes unity, direction, and friendship itself — two sides meeting at a perfect point.

What You'll Learn

Forward and backward knots

Creating mirrored symmetry

Meeting threads at the center

Materials

6 strands of embroidery floss (two of each color, cut 30–40 inches each)

Tape, clipboard, or safety pin

Scissors

Setup

Tie an overhand knot about 2 inches from the top to form your loop.

Secure your bracelet to your workspace.

Arrange your threads symmetrically — for example:

Left side: Blue, Yellow, Pink

Right side: Pink, Yellow, Blue

Each side mirrors the other, setting the stage for that signature "V."

How to Make the Pattern

Start with the leftmost thread (Color 1).

Tie forward knots (two half-knots) over each thread to its right until you reach the middle.

Then, switch to the rightmost thread (matching Color 1 on the opposite side).

Tie backward knots over each thread to its left until you reach the middle.

When both working threads meet in the center, tie a forward knot (or sometimes a backward knot) to connect them.

That's one row of your chevron!

For the next row, start again with your new leftmost and rightmost threads (Color 2).

Repeat the same steps, always meeting at the center.

As you progress, you'll see the elegant V-shapes stacking neatly, each row reinforcing your control and precision.

Tips for Success

Keep the center knot tight but not stiff; it's the anchor of your pattern.

If your chevrons look uneven, your tension may differ between sides — try pulling evenly on both.

Mirror your movements — for every forward knot on the left, there's a backward knot on the right.

Reflection

The chevron pattern teaches patience and symmetry — qualities that carry beyond the craft table. It's a perfect metaphor for balance: two sides working together in harmony to create beauty.

3. The Diagonal Dots Pattern

Once you're comfortable with the rhythm of forward and backward knots, it's time to introduce a little creativity! The Diagonal Dots Pattern is a cheerful variation that adds visual interest and texture. Instead of continuous lines, this pattern features small, colored "dots" that peek through the main background color — almost like confetti on fabric.

What You'll Learn

Switching directions mid-row

Controlled tension changes

Working with contrasting colors

Materials

5–6 strands of embroidery floss (choose one main background color and 2–3 accent colors)

Tape or clipboard

Scissors

Setup

Tie a loop and secure your bracelet.

Arrange your threads so your background color is placed between each accent color.

Example: Blue (background), Pink, Blue, Yellow, Blue, Green, Blue

How to Make the Pattern

Begin like a candy stripe, using the leftmost background thread as your working thread.

Make forward knots across the first few threads (usually 2–3).

When you reach an accent color thread, instead of tying over it, tie a backward knot on it.

This small reversal causes the accent color to "pop" through as a visible dot.

Continue the row, alternating directions whenever you want a new "dot" to appear.

Repeat this across each row, keeping your background color dominant but allowing small bursts of your accent colors to shine through.

Tips for Success

Plan your dot placement before starting. You can sketch it out as a guide.

Keep your knots slightly looser when switching directions to avoid puckering.

Use bright or metallic accent threads for a lively look.

Reflection

The diagonal dots pattern is a joyful reminder that perfection isn't the goal — playfulness is. It invites you to experiment, break repetition, and celebrate creativity. Every "dot" adds personality to your bracelet, making it truly one of a kind.

4. Braided and Twisted Ties — The Perfect Finish

Once you've completed a few inches of pattern, it's time to finish your bracelet neatly. The ties at the ends are just as important as the knots in the middle — they not only secure the bracelet on your wrist but also add a polished touch.

Here are two simple and elegant finishing techniques:

A. Braided Ties

Divide your remaining threads into three even groups.

Braid them just as you would hair — left over middle, right over middle — until you reach your desired length (about 3 inches).

Tie a simple knot at the end of the braid to secure it.

Repeat on the other side of your bracelet if you started with a loop.

Braided ties are strong, balanced, and look beautifully clean. You can even add a small bead at the end of each braid for decoration.

B. Twisted Ties

Twisted ties give a sleek, rope-like appearance and are incredibly easy to make.

Split your threads into two equal groups.

Twist each group tightly in the same direction (for example, clockwise).

Once both are tightly twisted, twist the two groups together in the opposite direction (counterclockwise).

Tie a small knot at the end to secure.

Twisted ties hold their shape beautifully and give a modern touch to your handmade bracelets.

Finishing Touches

To prevent fraying, apply a dab of fabric glue or clear nail polish to the ends of your knots. Allow them to dry fully before wearing. This small step ensures your bracelet stays neat and durable.

Practice, Patience, and Progress

Mastering these beginner patterns is like learning the basic strokes of painting. The more you practice, the more fluid and natural your movements become. Each pattern teaches something unique:

Candy Stripe develops rhythm.

Chevron teaches balance and mirroring.

Diagonal Dots encourages creativity and color play.

Braided Ties reinforce finishing discipline and neatness.

Remember, every bracelet you make — even the slightly crooked or uneven ones — is part of your artistic evolution. Over time, your hands will move intuitively, your knots will even out, and your confidence will bloom.

So, take your time. Savor each knot. Let the threads glide between your fingers as your mind relaxes and your creativity awakens.

Each bracelet isn't just a craft — it's a quiet meditation in color, patience, and friendship.

Chapter 5

Adding Personality — Beads, Charms, and Color Choices

Now that you've learned how to knot, weave, and create your first few friendship bracelet patterns, it's time to explore what makes your bracelets truly yours. The joy of friendship bracelet making is not only in the rhythm of tying knots but in the freedom of expression — the way each piece reflects personality, emotion, and intention.

Adding your personal touch transforms a simple bracelet into a meaningful keepsake. Whether it's through carefully chosen colors, symbolic charms, or decorative beads, every choice you make adds character and story to your creation.

In this chapter, we'll explore how to use color psychology to express emotions, how to incorporate beads and charms into your designs, and how to balance creativity with craftsmanship to make your bracelets stand out as unique works of wearable art.

The Power of Color — Expressing Emotion Through Thread

Colors are not just visual — they are emotional, symbolic, and deeply personal. Every shade you choose carries an energy that can convey messages without words. When you make a friendship bracelet, you're essentially painting with thread. The colors you use tell a story, set a mood, and speak from the heart.

Here's a simple guide to help you choose colors with meaning and intention:

Blue – Trust and Peace

Blue represents calm, stability, and honesty. It's the color of the sky and the ocean — soothing, expansive, and tranquil. A blue bracelet makes a beautiful gift for a loyal friend or someone going through a stressful time. It carries a sense of comfort and serenity.

Red – Passion and Courage

Red is the color of energy, strength, and love. It's bold and vibrant, representing passion, determination, and warmth. Red bracelets make heartfelt tokens for those who inspire you, or as a reminder to embrace courage and confidence in your own life.

Green – Growth and Harmony

Green connects us to nature. It's the color of renewal, balance, and abundance. A green bracelet can symbolize fresh starts, personal growth, or a friendship that continues to flourish over time. It's also grounding — a wonderful choice for someone who brings calm to your life.

Yellow – Joy and Optimism

Yellow radiates happiness, positivity, and creativity. Like sunshine, it uplifts the spirit. A yellow bracelet brings a smile to anyone's day, symbolizing laughter, hope, and gratitude. It's perfect for celebrating cheerful personalities or marking joyful milestones.

Purple – Imagination and Wisdom

Purple is the color of mystery, creativity, and inner strength. Historically associated with royalty and spirituality, it represents insight and inspiration. Use purple to create bracelets that feel thoughtful and empowering.

Pink – Love and Kindness

Soft and gentle, pink is often linked to affection and compassion. A pink bracelet can express care, warmth, and emotional closeness — ideal for best friends, siblings, or romantic partners.

Orange – Energy and Enthusiasm

Orange combines the strength of red and the joy of yellow. It's dynamic, energetic, and full of life. A great choice for someone adventurous, optimistic, or always on the move!

White – Purity and New Beginnings

White symbolizes simplicity, clarity, and peace. It's a versatile color that pairs beautifully with others, adding balance and light. A white bracelet can represent hope, mindfulness, or starting fresh.

Black – Strength and Sophistication

Black adds depth, grounding, and a touch of elegance. It can represent protection, resilience, or inner strength. Paired with brighter colors, it creates contrast and visual balance.

Color Combinations — Telling a Story with Shades

While single colors carry individual meanings, the real magic happens when you combine them. Just like emotions, colors interact and influence each other. A well-thought-out color palette can make your bracelet feel harmonious, expressive, and powerful.

Here are some ideas to inspire your combinations:

The Calm Set: Blue, white, and green — for balance, peace, and healing.

The Energy Burst: Red, orange, and yellow — for positivity and motivation.

The Dreamer's Mix: Purple, pink, and silver — for imagination and creativity.

The Nature Lover: Green, brown, and gold — for grounding and renewal.

The Minimalist: Black, grey, and white — for elegance and clarity.

Don't be afraid to experiment. Sometimes the most unexpected color pairings produce the most beautiful results. Trust your instincts — if it feels good, it will look good.

Adding Beads — Sparkle, Texture, and Dimension

Once you're comfortable with your basic knotting patterns, beads are a wonderful way to add personality and texture to your friendship bracelets. They give your designs a touch of sparkle, a bit of movement, and endless creative possibilities.

Types of Beads

Seed Beads: Tiny, round, and versatile — perfect for subtle accents.

Letter Beads: Great for personalizing your bracelet with names, initials, or meaningful words.

Glass Beads: Add shimmer and elegance, ideal for decorative designs.

Wooden Beads: Earthy and rustic, great for natural or boho styles.

Metal or Gemstone Beads: Add sophistication, weight, and symbolic meaning (e.g., rose quartz for love, amethyst for calm).

When to Add Beads

You can add beads during the knotting process or after finishing your bracelet.

During knotting: Slide a bead onto the working thread before making your next knot. This embeds the bead neatly into the design.

After knotting: Thread beads onto the bracelet ends and secure them with a knot or a small dab of fabric glue or clear nail polish.

Pro Tip: If your beads have small holes, use a fine needle to help thread them. Waxing your embroidery floss with a little candle wax can also make it easier to pass through tight spaces.

Incorporating Charms — Meaningful Little Details

Charms bring a touch of storytelling to your bracelets. Each charm carries a symbol — a tiny expression of intention or memory.

Popular Charm Symbols

Heart: Love and affection

Star: Hope and inspiration

Feather: Freedom and spiritual growth

Tree: Strength and rootedness

Butterfly: Transformation and new beginnings

Infinity Symbol: Eternal friendship

Anchor: Stability and support

Attach charms using small jump rings (tiny metal loops) or tie them directly into your bracelet as you knot. You can position them at the center for a focal point or at the ends for subtle detailing.

Pro Tip: Choose charms that resonate with your bracelet's color theme or emotional intention. For example, a blue bracelet with a star charm could represent hope and peace.

Personalizing Your Bracelets

The true beauty of friendship bracelets lies in their personalization. You're not just crafting jewelry — you're creating a connection, a keepsake that holds emotion. Here are some creative ways to make your bracelets one of a kind:

Add initials or names using letter beads.

Create thematic designs — for example, a "sunset bracelet" using orange, pink, and purple threads.

Incorporate birthstones or zodiac charms for astrological flair.

Use texture contrast by mixing matte, metallic, and glossy threads.

Attach a tassel or small bell at the end for a whimsical finish.

Each element tells a story — about who you are, who you're creating for, and what you wish to express.

Chapter 6

FRIENDSHIP BRACELET PROJECTS

Project 1 — Classic Candy Stripe Bracelet

76

Skill level: Beginner

You'll practice: Forward knots, color order, tension control

Materials

6 strands embroidery floss (6 different colors), 35 in / 90 cm each

Scissors, measuring tape

Tape, clipboard, or safety pin for anchoring

Optional: small bead or button for closure; fabric glue/clear nail polish

Prep

Cut & fold: Align the 6 strands, fold in half to find the midpoint.

Top loop: Tie an overhand knot about 2 in / 5 cm below the fold to form a loop.

Anchor: Secure the loop to your surface (tape/clipboard/pin).

Arrange colors: Lay threads flat left-to-right in the stripe order you want (e.g., red, orange, yellow, green, blue, purple). This is the exact order the stripes will appear, repeating.

Knot Language Refresher

Forward knot (FK): Working thread is on the left; form a "4" over the neighbor, pull end under and up; tighten twice (two half-knots = one full knot). Each FK moves the working thread one position right.

Step-by-Step

Row 1 starter: Take the leftmost thread (Color 1).

Cross the row: Tie FK over each thread to its right, one by one, until Color 1 reaches the far right.

Row 2 starter: The new leftmost thread is now Color 2. Repeat: tie FK across the row to the far right.

Repeat rhythm: Always start with the current leftmost thread, FK across, park on right. Rows stack into diagonal stripes.

Finishing

When the patterned length equals wrist size minus ½ in / 1.2 cm, stop.

Tie a tight overhand knot under the last row.

Ties: Split ends into either two groups (twist) or three groups (braid) for 2–3 in / 5–7.5 cm and knot the tips.

Add a dab of glue to the end knots.

Fit & Closure Options

Loop + end knot: Use the top loop and a bottom knot to fasten.

Button/bead: Thread all ends through a bead/button, knot under it; the bead passes through the top loop.

Troubleshooting

Curving right: Knots are too tight. Loosen slightly on next few rows.

Jagged edges: Inconsistent tension. Hold base thread taut and slide knots up gently before tightening.

Gaps between rows: Slide each half-knot snugly to the top before tightening the second half.

Quick Variations

Mini stripe: Use 4 strands (2 colors doubled).

Double stripe: Place duplicate colors side-by-side (e.g., red, red, orange, orange...).

Ombre: Arrange same-family shades light→dark.

Project 2 — Chevron Bracelet

Skill level: Beginner–Intermediate

You'll practice: Forward knots (left side), backward knots (right side), meeting cleanly at center

Materials

6 colors (cut 35–40 in / 90–100 cm each), then double them to 12 strands for bold chevrons

Scissors, tape/clipboard/pin, measuring tape

Optional: bead/button closure; glue

Prep

Cut & double: For 6 colors, cut one strand each, fold to double—now 12 working threads.

Top loop: Tie an overhand knot 2 in / 5 cm from fold to form loop; anchor.

Mirror order layout: Arrange threads symmetrically around the center:
A B C D E F | F E D C B A
(The bar is the center line.)

Knot Language

Forward knot (FK): Left thread over right neighbor; moves right.

Backward knot (BK): Right thread over left neighbor; moves left.

Center knot: When left and right working threads meet, tie one FK (or BK—pick one and stay consistent).

Step-by-Step

Left sweep: Take leftmost thread (A on left). FK over each neighbor to the middle.

Right sweep: Take rightmost matching thread (A on right). BK over each neighbor to the middle.

Center join: Tie a single FK (or BK) to join the two A's at center. One row completed.

Next color: Repeat with B threads: left side FK to center; right side BK to center; join.

Continue sequence: Work C, D, E, F in the same fashion, then the flow cycles back to A again as colors rotate outward→inward.

Finishing

As with Project 1: stop at length, secure with an overhand knot, add braided/twisted ties, seal ends.

Clean Centerline Tips

Even tension both sides: If the V is skewed, you're pulling harder on one side—match the feel of your pull.

Consistent center knot: Always use the same knot type (FK or BK) at the center for a crisp spine.

Tidy stack: After each center join, lightly press the row upward to close micro-gaps.

Troubleshooting

Left V higher than right: Right-side BKs are too loose or left-side FKs too tight—balance tension.

Center hole: Pull the center join snug, but don't yank. Practice a smooth upward slide, then tighten.

Quick Variations

Skinny chevron: Use 8 strands instead of 12.

Double chevron: Keep duplicate colors adjacent on both sides (A A B B C C | C C B B A A) to create "double lines."

Gradient V: Arrange light→dark on each side for shaded arrows.

Project 3 — Diamond Pattern Bracelet

Skill level: Intermediate

You'll practice: Switching directions within rows, controlled FBK/BFK knots, "opening" and "closing" shapes

Diamonds are built by chevron logic plus controlled direction changes to form the diamond outline and the inner "window." You can keep the inside empty (open diamond), fill it with a color, or place a bead.

Materials

8–12 strands embroidery floss, 40 in / 100 cm each (more strands = larger diamonds)

Scissors, tape/clipboard/pin, measuring tape

Optional: size 6/0–8/0 seed beads for diamond centers; glue

Prep

Loop & anchor: Tie a loop as before (2 in / 5 cm from top); secure.

Symmetry layout: Use a mirrored setup like the chevron:

For 8 strands: A B C D | D C B A

For 12 strands: A B C D E F | F E D C B A

Choose A as outline color for diamonds (high-contrast), B–F as fills/background.

Knot Language

FK/BK: as before.

FBK (forward-backward): Start FK then BK— keeps the working thread on left side after a rightward interaction.

BFK (backward-forward): Start BK then FK— keeps working thread on right side after a leftward interaction.

These two "pivot" knots help you reverse direction smoothly to draw diamond corners.

Outline Logic (One Diamond Cycle)

A full diamond usually spans 6–10 rows depending on width. Think in four phases: open top, expand sides, close bottom, reset.

Phase 1 — Open the Top Point

Row 1 (chevron base): Work like Project 2: A left FK to center, A right BK to center, join at center. This creates the top point of the diamond in color A.

Phase 2 — Expand the Sides

Row 2:

Left side: Work B over C with FK until just before the center where A should "frame." Use FBK when you want A to stop advancing and hold its position as outline.

Right side mirrors the left: Use BFK to keep A in place on the right while other colors approach.
Goal: A threads step outward one row at a time, drawing the slanted edges of the diamond. FBK/BFK let you pivot without sending A across the row.

Rows 3–4: Continue expanding using FK/BK for background and FBK/BFK pivots at the points where the outline color A must change direction and remain at the edge of the diamond. You'll see a hollow diamond shape growing.

Phase 3 — Close the Bottom Point

Rows 5–6: Start bringing the sides inward:

Left side: where A needs to angle inward, use the opposite pivot so A travels back toward center (e.g., if you were holding A in place with FBK, now you'll resume standard FKs or mirror with BKs depending on side).

Right side mirrors.
When the two A threads meet at the center again, join with a single FK (or BK). You've created the bottom point.

Phase 4 — Reset

Rows 7–8: Work a row or two of standard chevron (or your background color) to space diamonds, then repeat Phases 1–3 for the next diamond.

Tip: If this feels abstract, mark on paper where the outline color A should appear each row; your knot choices merely "park" or "move" A to those coordinates.

Filling the Diamond

Open (hollow) diamond: Keep interior knots in background colors; pivot A only at edges.

Solid diamond: Once the sides are established, carry color A inside using standard FK/BK to fill rows between the outlines.

Beaded center: When your outline forms a small window at mid-diamond, slide a bead onto the center pair before joining; lock it with the next row's knots.

Step-by-Step (8-Strand Example)

Row 1: A left FK to center; A right BK to center; join—top point made.

Row 2: On left, work B over C with FK until A should remain at edge—use FBK with A to pivot and hold; on right mirror with BFK.

Rows 3–4: Continue expanding edges: whenever A reaches a corner, pivot (FBK/BFK) to "trace" the outline; keep background colors crossing beneath.

Rows 5–6: Bring outlines inward; stop using pivots and resume traveling A toward center with standard FK/BK; join at center—bottom point made.

Rows 7–8: Optional spacer rows (plain chevron or background). Repeat cycle.

Finishing

Tie off, add braided/twisted ties or bead/button closure, seal knots as in prior projects.

Troubleshooting

Squashed diamond: Too few expansion rows—add one more row of outward pivots before closing.

Leaning diamond: Uneven tension between sides—count rows on each side and match your pull.

Outline gaps: Pivot knots (FBK/BFK) not snug—slide each half-knot up before tightening the second half.

Designer Variations

Alternating colors: Switch the outline color A every diamond.

Nested diamonds: After completing one large diamond, start a smaller one immediately inside by pivoting sooner.

Two-tone background: Use left-side background cool tones, right-side warm tones for dramatic contrast.

Project 4 – Zigzag Bracelet

Skill Level: Intermediate

You'll Learn: Direction changes, color alternation, pattern rhythm

The Zigzag Bracelet is a lively, energetic pattern that plays with direction. Its eye-catching wavy lines look complex, but once you master the flow, it becomes meditative and satisfying to knot. The magic comes from alternating forward and backward knots—creating gentle bends that form the illusion of a wave or "zigzag" moving across the bracelet.

Materials

8 strands of embroidery floss (2 strands of each of 4 colors)

Each strand about 35–40 inches (90–100 cm) long

Scissors, measuring tape

Tape, clipboard, or safety pin

Optional: small charm or bead for the center or closure

Setup

Cut and fold your threads as usual, fold them in half, and tie an overhand knot about 2 inches (5 cm) from the top to create a loop.

Arrange the threads symmetrically from the center outward in repeating color order. For example:
A B C D | D C B A
(This mirrored setup helps maintain balance on both sides.)

Secure your loop to the workspace with tape, pin, or clipboard.

Step-by-Step Instructions

Start the left side: Take the leftmost thread (A) and make forward knots over each thread to the center. Stop when you reach the middle.

Now the right side: Take the rightmost thread (A) and make backward knots over each thread to the center, where it meets the other A.

Join in the center using a single forward knot (FK) to complete the first V shape — similar to the chevron pattern.

Reverse direction: Here's where the "zigzag" starts! On the next row, instead of continuing in the same direction, you'll now mirror the knot flow.

Take the leftmost thread again (B), but now begin by tying backward knots toward the outer edge.

On the right side, take B and tie forward knots toward the right edge.

This reversal creates a "bend" or change in direction, forming the zigzag motion.

Continue this alternating flow — one row inward (chevron-like), one row outward (reverse chevron). You'll see smooth, rhythmic waves appearing across your bracelet.

Tips for Perfect Zigzags

Mark reversal rows: Place a tiny pencil dot or removable tape marker every few rows to remind yourself where to switch directions.

Consistent tension: Pull knots evenly. Over-tightening will distort the curves.

Smooth transitions: When changing direction, hold the threads taut but relaxed to prevent sharp kinks.

Finishing

When the bracelet reaches the desired length:

Tie an overhand knot beneath the last row.

Create braided or twisted ends for 2–3 inches (5–7.5 cm).

Apply a dab of clear nail polish or glue to secure the final knots.

Creative Variations

Rainbow Zigzag: Use a full spectrum of colors for a playful look.

Two-tone Waves: Alternate just two colors for a minimal, graphic effect.

Gradient Effect: Arrange shades of one color (like ocean blues) from light to dark, enhancing the illusion of movement.

Charm Detail: Attach a tiny charm or bead at the bottom to emphasize the "wave's endpoint."

The Zigzag Bracelet teaches fluid control of direction — an essential foundation for more advanced geometric and curved designs later on.

Project 5 – Heart Pattern Bracelet: Perfect for Gifts

Skill Level: Intermediate

You'll Learn: Center-shape formation, mirroring technique, and symbolic design

Few friendship bracelet designs are as beloved as the Heart Pattern. It's the perfect gift for a friend, partner, or family member — a small, meaningful token tied with affection. The repeating hearts look intricate but rely entirely on clever arrangement and mirrored knotting.

Materials

12 strands of embroidery floss (6 colors, doubled) — 35–40 inches (90–100 cm) each

Scissors, measuring tape

Tape, clipboard, or safety pin

Optional: a single metallic thread for "highlight hearts"

Setup

Cut and fold strands, tie an overhand knot about 2 inches from the fold for your loop.

Arrange threads in mirror order on both sides, like this:

A B C D E F | F E D C B A

Choose A as your background color and F as your heart color.

Understanding the Pattern

This bracelet is based on the chevron foundation, but you'll strategically switch knot directions to make small "valleys" in the rows that form the top curves of the heart. The center join of each heart happens when two colored threads meet in the middle.

Step-by-Step Instructions

Base Rows (Background): Start by making 2–3 rows of plain chevron using your background color (A). This sets up your canvas.

Begin the Heart:

Take F (heart color) on both the left and right sides.

On the left, use forward knots (FK) moving inward. On the right, use backward knots (BK) moving inward.

Meet the two F threads in the middle with a single FK (or BK). This forms the heart's bottom point.

Forming the Top Arches:

In the next few rows, use FBK (forward-backward) and BFK (backward-forward) knots to pivot the heart threads outward, creating the curve at the top of the heart.

This part creates two small bumps resembling the top of a heart shape.

Background Fills: Use your background threads (A–E) to fill the space around the heart, making it stand out clearly.

Repeat: After finishing one heart, add two background rows (A) before starting the next heart.

Helpful Hints

Symmetry is key: Always count rows on both sides to keep heart shapes even.

Heart color dominance: Make sure your heart color threads don't twist under other threads — they must stay visible on top.

Smooth arches: Keep pivot knots snug but not tight; this prevents sharp points.

Finishing

When the bracelet is long enough:

End with a few rows of background color to "frame" the last heart.

Tie an overhand knot.

Braid or twist the ends and finish with glue or clear nail polish.

Creative Variations

Double Hearts: Use two heart-color threads on each side for thicker, bolder hearts.

Gradient Love: Use shades from pink to red for romantic fade effects.

Rainbow Hearts: Each heart a different color — joyful and perfect for friends or Pride gifts.

Message Accent: Add a letter bead or charm between hearts with initials or symbols.

Gifting Ideas

The Heart Pattern Bracelet is perfect for birthdays, anniversaries, Valentine's Day, or simply as a way to say "thank you" or "I care." Pair it with a small handwritten card explaining that each knot represents love, patience, and connection — turning your handmade bracelet into a keepsake.

Project 6 – Wave Pattern Bracelet:
Flowing Ocean-Inspired Look

Skill Level: Intermediate to Advanced Beginner

You'll Learn: Alternating thread layering, soft curve transitions, and blended color harmony

The Wave Pattern Bracelet captures the soothing movement of the ocean. It's a beautifully fluid design that flows gracefully across the wrist — perfect for anyone drawn to nature, calm energy, and organic forms. You'll use alternating forward and backward knots, similar to the Zigzag, but with layered colors that "roll" into each other like gentle waves.

Materials

10 strands of embroidery floss (2 strands each of 5 shades of blue or green)

Each strand about 40 inches (100 cm) long

Scissors, measuring tape

Tape or clipboard for securing

Optional: clear seed beads for sparkle, matching charm (e.g., seashell or pearl)

Setup

Cut and fold: Prepare strands and tie a loop about 2 inches (5 cm) from the top.

Arrange by gradient: Lightest shade on the outside, progressing to darkest in the center, then mirror order on the right: Light–Medium–Dark–Medium–Light | Light–Medium–Dark–Medium–Light

Secure your loop to your workspace.

Step-by-Step Instructions

Start left to right: Begin with your outermost light blue thread. Make forward knots (FK) across each of the next four threads to the center.

Start right to left: Take the outermost thread on the right and make backward knots (BK) across to the center.

Center join: Tie a single FK (or BK) to complete the first chevron-style row.

Shift the wave: For the next row, start again from the leftmost thread, but this time, stop one knot earlier — this leaves one thread "behind" to start forming a dip.

Mirror the movement: On the right side, do the same — stop one knot short of the middle. You'll notice a gentle curve starting to form.

Continue shifting: Each row alternates how far you go before stopping, creating rolling curves.

Color layering: As you progress, threads will naturally change positions. This movement between lighter and darker threads enhances the flowing, wavelike illusion.

Once you reach mid-pattern: Reverse the direction of the waves by increasing the number of knots again — this "brings the waves back up," just like the ocean's ebb and flow.

Tips for Perfect Waves

Use gradient colors: The smoother the transition between shades, the more natural the wave effect.

Maintain tension balance: Keep knots snug but not tight; overly tight knots create angular rather than curved lines.

Smooth rolling effect: Try to move one thread fewer or one thread extra per row for a more pronounced ripple.

Optional shimmer: Add a subtle bead between sections to mimic glimmering sunlight on water.

Finishing

When you've reached the desired length:

Tie an overhand knot beneath the last row.

Add braided ties about 3 inches long.

Optionally, attach a small ocean-themed charm (like a shell or fish) for a personal touch.

Creative Variations

Sunset Waves: Swap blues for yellows, pinks, and oranges — the result resembles evening waves under a sunset sky.

Monochrome Motion: Use one color in different tones (light to dark blue or green) for a sophisticated, subtle effect.

Beaded Surf: Thread clear or white beads randomly through the pattern to represent foam or bubbles.

Mixed Texture: Try combining embroidery floss with metallic or hemp threads to add shimmer and texture.

Meaning Behind the Design

The Wave Pattern Bracelet symbolizes flow, peace, and renewal — qualities inspired by the sea. Many crafters find the repetitive motion of tying these smooth, wave-like patterns deeply meditative. It's an excellent bracelet for mindfulness practice or as a calming project after a long day.

Pro Crafter's Tip

To create a double wave effect:

Use 14 strands instead of 10, alternating two gradient sequences (e.g., light blue → dark blue → light green → dark green).

Work each "wave" to meet at the centerline, giving the bracelet twin flowing curves — perfect for ocean lovers.

Project 7 — Beaded Ladder Bracelet: Adds Shimmer with Beads

Skill Level: Intermediate

You'll Learn: Threading beads, ladder weaving, maintaining structure and symmetry

Overview

The Beaded Ladder Bracelet combines the softness of thread with the sparkle of beads, creating a modern twist on the traditional friendship bracelet. This design resembles a delicate ladder — colorful cords form the "rails," while beads act as the "rungs," connecting each side in a shimmering rhythm.

This bracelet is especially popular as a gift because it looks sophisticated yet is surprisingly easy to make once you understand the weaving technique.

Materials

2 strands of embroidery floss (for the side rails) — each about 40 inches (100 cm) long

1 contrasting color strand (for weaving) — 60 inches (150 cm) long

A set of small seed beads or glass beads (size 6/0 or 8/0 works best)

Needle (thin beading needle)

Scissors

Tape or clipboard

Optional: clear nail polish or glue to seal ends

Setup

Cut your threads: Cut the two outer "rail" threads (40 inches each) and the weaving thread (60 inches).

Secure the rails: Tie the two side threads together at the top using an overhand knot, leaving a 2-inch (5 cm) tail for later braiding. Tape or pin the knot securely to your workspace.

Prepare the weaver thread: Tie the center of the long weaving thread just below the knot, so both ends hang down evenly. These two ends will alternate to pass through the beads.

Step-by-Step Instructions

Thread the needle with the left end of your weaving thread.

Add your first bead: Slide one bead onto the left thread and position it between the two rail threads.

Anchor the bead: Pass the right thread through the same bead in the opposite direction, forming a "loop" that traps the bead horizontally between the two rails. Pull both threads snugly so the bead sits tight and centered.

Repeat the process: Add another bead to the left thread, pass the right thread through from the other side, and tighten. You'll see the ladder shape forming row by row.

Continue weaving: Keep adding beads until the bracelet reaches the desired length.

Tips for a Perfect Ladder

Consistent tension: Keep both weaving threads taut so the beads align evenly.

Use even-sized beads: Irregular beads will cause the ladder to wobble.

Spacing: Pull gently but firmly to ensure each bead sits close without overlapping.

Finishing

Once you reach your desired length, tie all threads together in a secure knot just below the last bead.

Braid or twist the ends into ties.

Apply a drop of clear nail polish or glue to reinforce the knots.

Creative Variations

Two-tone rails: Use different colors for the side threads.

Patterned beads: Alternate bead colors for striped or rainbow effects.

Add a charm: Attach a tiny pendant or crystal in the center for extra sparkle.

Metallic mix: Use metallic or pearl beads for a glamorous look.

Quick Tip

If you don't have a beading needle, stiffen the ends of your thread with clear nail polish or beeswax — this makes threading through beads easier.

The Beaded Ladder Bracelet is elegant, versatile, and perfect for anyone who loves mixing textures. It adds shimmer and dimension while staying true to the handmade charm of friendship bracelets.

Project 8 — Double Chevron Bracelet: Layered Symmetry with Rich Color Depth

Skill Level: Intermediate

You'll Learn: Layering colors, mirroring patterns, mastering complex symmetry

Overview

The Double Chevron Bracelet is a stunning upgrade from the basic chevron. It's richer, more detailed, and visually dynamic — featuring two mirrored V-shapes per color sequence. This layering gives your bracelet depth and a professional finish. Once you've mastered the regular chevron (Project 2), this is your next step.

Materials

6 colors of embroidery floss (cut 40 inches / 100 cm each), doubled to create 12 working strands

Scissors, measuring tape

Tape, clipboard, or safety pin

Optional: bead or button for closure

Setup

Cut 6 colors of thread and fold them in half; tie an overhand knot 2 inches (5 cm) from the top to make a loop.

Arrange the threads in a mirror order on both sides, like this:
A A B B C C | C C B B A A
(Each pair will form the double chevron lines.)

Secure the loop to your workspace.

Step-by-Step Instructions

Left side: Take the outermost thread on the left (A). Tie forward knots over both A threads to its right — one at a time — until it reaches the center.

Right side: Take the outermost thread on the right (A). Tie backward knots over both threads to the left until it meets the center.

Center join: Tie the two A threads together using one FK (forward knot).

Next color (B): Repeat the same process with the next color pair.

Left B thread → FK toward center

Right B thread → BK toward center

Join the Bs at center

Continue this pattern: C follows next, forming layered double chevrons.

Each double line of color creates depth, giving your bracelet a "3D" look.

Advanced Variation (Triple Chevron)

If you're confident, you can expand to triple color layers by placing three of each color on both sides. It requires the same knot rhythm, just more strands per side.

Tips for Precision

Even spacing: Pull knots snugly to maintain symmetry.

Thread management: Clip stray strands to keep them tangle-free.

Row consistency: Keep count of each row so color transitions stay balanced.

Finishing

When your bracelet reaches the desired length, tie an overhand knot below the last row.

Braid or twist the tails into two neat ties.

Secure with glue or nail polish.

Creative Variations

Gradient Effect: Use shades of one color family — light to dark blues, pinks, or greens.

Bold Contrast: Alternate complementary colors (e.g., red and green, purple and yellow).

Beaded Edges: Thread small metallic beads onto the outer strands before knotting for subtle sparkle.

The Double Chevron Bracelet radiates craftsmanship — it's a showstopper that combines geometry, color layering, and steady technique.

Project 9 — Spiral Twist Bracelet: Quick and Elegant

Skill Level: Beginner–Intermediate

You'll Learn: Spiral technique, consistent tension, clean twisting motion

Overview

The Spiral Twist Bracelet is one of the simplest yet most elegant friendship bracelets you can make. It's quick, minimal, and looks beautiful alone or stacked with others. This project uses forward knots only, which naturally creates a spiral effect as the threads twist together.

Materials

4 strands of embroidery floss (2 colors works well) — each 40 inches (100 cm) long

Scissors, measuring tape

Tape or clipboard

Setup

Cut your four strands, align them, and fold in half.

Tie an overhand knot 2 inches (5 cm) below the fold for a loop.

Secure the loop to your workspace.

Arrange threads in your preferred order.

Step-by-Step Instructions

Take the leftmost thread (your working thread).

Form a forward knot (FK) over the next thread to the right. Tighten gently.

Using the same working thread, continue making forward knots over each remaining thread until it reaches the far right.

Don't change direction — return the same working thread to the leftmost position and repeat the process.

As you continue knotting in this one direction, you'll notice the bracelet naturally begins to twist into a beautiful spiral.

Tips for Perfect Spirals

Consistent tension: The tighter your knots, the tighter your spiral. Slightly loosen tension for a relaxed, rope-like look.

Thread colors: For a two-tone spiral, alternate colors in your setup.

Avoid tangling: Occasionally untwist your bracelet from the base if it starts to curl too tightly.

Finishing

Once you've reached your desired length, tie an overhand knot beneath the final row.

Divide the ends into two pairs, twist or braid them for ties.

Seal with glue or clear polish.

Creative Variations

Rainbow Twist: Use multiple bright colors for a lively effect.

Thick Rope: Use 6–8 strands instead of 4 for a chunkier look.

Metallic Accent: Replace one thread with metallic embroidery floss for subtle shine.

Why It Works

Because every knot is tied in one direction, the bracelet curls naturally — no extra effort needed. This makes it one of the most beginner-friendly designs, ideal for quick projects, gifts, or layered bracelet stacks.

Project 10 — Personalized Name Bracelet: Spell It Out!

Skill Level: Intermediate

You'll Learn: Bead integration, text alignment, personalization

Overview

The Personalized Name Bracelet transforms a simple friendship bracelet into a meaningful keepsake. Whether you spell a friend's name, a motivational word, or a short message, this bracelet becomes uniquely personal —

perfect for birthdays, friendship gifts, or team spirit accessories.

Materials

6 strands of embroidery floss — 35–40 inches (90–100 cm) each

A set of alphabet beads (plastic, acrylic, or wooden)

A needle (if bead holes are small)

Scissors

Tape or clipboard

Optional: heart or star beads for decoration

Setup

Cut and align your threads, fold in half, and tie a loop about 2 inches (5 cm) from the top.

Arrange colors however you prefer — consider using one neutral background color and one accent color to make the name stand out.

Secure your bracelet to your workspace.

Step-by-Step Instructions

Start the base: Begin with 6–8 rows of plain Candy Stripe or Chevron pattern to create a base.

Thread your first letter bead: Once ready, bring the two center threads together and slide the bead onto them.

Anchor the bead: Tie an overhand knot just below the bead to keep it secure and centered.

Continue the pattern: Add a few rows of standard knots after the bead before adding the next letter bead.

Repeat for each letter: Space beads evenly — about 2–3 rows apart for best visibility.

Finish the bracelet with a few rows of knots after the last bead for balance.

Tips for Alignment

Centered placement: If the name has an odd number of letters, start the first bead slightly above the midpoint so it centers when worn.

Tighten gently: Pull thread evenly when securing beads — too much tension may warp alignment.

Pre-plan spacing: Lay out your beads in order before starting.

Finishing

Tie an overhand knot beneath the last bead row.

Braid or twist the ends into ties.

Seal knots with glue

Chapter 7

Finishing and Wearing

You've come so far — from learning your first knots to mastering intricate patterns and personal designs. Now it's time for one of the most satisfying parts of the bracelet-making journey: finishing and caring for your creations.

How you finish your bracelet determines both how it looks and how well it lasts. A clean, sturdy finish makes your bracelet comfortable to wear, easy to remove, and durable enough to stand the test of time. After all, your handmade bracelet isn't just a craft — it's a piece of wearable art and emotion.

In this chapter, we'll explore several ways to finish your bracelets beautifully, ensure they fit comfortably, and learn how to care for them so they remain vibrant and strong for years to come.

The Art of Finishing — Giving Your Bracelet a Professional Touch

When you've completed knotting your bracelet and reached your desired length, you may be tempted to tie a quick knot and snip the ends — but taking a few extra minutes to finish it properly will make a world of difference.

A thoughtful finish not only improves appearance but also enhances wearability. It allows you to adjust the fit, prevents fraying, and makes your bracelet easy to put on and take off.

Here are some of the most popular and effective ways to finish your friendship bracelets:

1. Loop and Knot Closure (Classic and Reliable)

The loop and knot closure is the most traditional and sturdy method for finishing friendship bracelets. It's ideal for everyday wear and perfect for bracelets you plan to gift or exchange.

How to Make It:

When you begin your bracelet, create a small loop (about half an inch) by folding your threads in half and tying an overhand knot near the fold. This will be your closure loop.

At the end of your bracelet, once you've reached the desired length, tie another overhand knot using all the threads together.

Leave about 2–3 inches of thread beyond the knot — this will allow you to braid or twist the ends if desired.

When wearing the bracelet, simply slip the end knot through the starting loop — it should fit snugly but comfortably.

Why It Works:

This closure is strong, simple, and doesn't require any extra materials. It's especially practical for bracelets you might tie on and leave for weeks — a true friendship bracelet tradition!

2. Button or Bead Closure (Stylish and Functional)

If you want your bracelet to stand out, consider finishing it with a button or bead closure. This adds a polished, jewelry-like touch while keeping it easy to wear and remove.

How to Make It:

Select a bead or button with a hole large enough for your threads to pass through.

At the end of your bracelet, thread all your strands through the button or bead.

Tie a secure overhand knot beneath it to hold it in place.

Make sure your starting loop is slightly larger than the bead or button so it can pass through easily but still hold securely once fastened.

Creative Tip:

Choose buttons or beads that complement your color scheme or theme. For example:

Wooden beads for natural, earthy designs.

Pearl or metallic beads for an elegant finish.

Brightly colored or patterned buttons for playful, youthful styles.

This closure not only makes your bracelet easier to put on but also adds a professional touch that elevates it from handmade to handcrafted.

3. Braided or Twisted Ends (Adjustable and Comfortable)

If you prefer flexibility, braided or twisted ends make a great finish. They're soft, adjustable, and give your bracelet a relaxed, bohemian look.

How to Make It:

Once you finish your bracelet, divide the loose ends into three equal sections.

Braid them tightly for 2–3 inches and tie a knot at the bottom.

Repeat on the other side if you began with a loop.

Alternatively, for a twisted finish:

Split the threads into two equal groups.

Twist each group individually in the same direction (clockwise).

Then twist both groups together in the opposite direction (counterclockwise).

Tie a knot to secure the twist.

These finishes are ideal for adjustable bracelets — you can tie them around your wrist and adjust the tightness easily.

4. Sliding Knot Closure (For Adjustable Fit)

For a modern, polished look, you can create a sliding knot closure, similar to what you see on store-bought cord bracelets. It allows the wearer to tighten or loosen the bracelet effortlessly.

How to Make It:

When your bracelet is finished, cross the two ends over each other.

Using one of the threads, tie a few square knots around both bracelet ends.

Pull the knots tight, trim excess thread, and seal the ends with glue.

When done correctly, the bracelet's ends will slide through the knots, making it adjustable and elegant. This style is great for selling or gifting, as it fits most wrist sizes.

Sealing and Securing Your Ends

No matter which closure you choose, it's essential to protect your bracelet from fraying. Embroidery floss and cotton threads are beautiful but can unravel over time, especially with regular wear.

To ensure longevity:

Dab a tiny bit of fabric glue or clear nail polish on the end knots.

Let it dry completely before wearing.

Avoid using too much — a light coating is enough to seal the fibers.

This simple step strengthens your knots and helps your bracelet withstand daily use without coming undone.

Chapter 11

Designing Your Own Patterns

By now, you've learned all the fundamental knots, techniques, and styles that form the heart of friendship bracelet making. You've tied diagonal stripes, woven chevrons, twisted spirals, and even added beads and names to personalize your designs. You've practiced tension, explored color harmony, and built skill through patience and joy.

Now, it's time for the most exciting part of your creative journey — designing your own patterns.

This chapter is all about freedom and imagination. Once you understand the building blocks of friendship bracelets — forward and backward knots — you have everything you need to create endless variations. Designing your own pattern transforms you from a learner into an artist. It's where your creativity takes the lead, and your personality begins to shine through each thread.

So, gather your favorite colors, grab a piece of graph paper (or an online pattern generator), and let's explore how to design bracelets that are as unique, expressive, and meaningful as you are.

Understanding the Anatomy of a Pattern

Before diving into design, let's revisit what a pattern really is.

A friendship bracelet pattern is a visual roadmap — a sequence of colored knots that guides you row by row. Each knot represents a small decision in your design: direction, color, and placement.

The four basic knots — forward (FK), backward (BK), forward-backward (FBK), and backward-forward (BFK) — form the entire language of bracelet patterns. Think of them as letters in an alphabet. Once you know the "letters," you can form your own "words" — or in this case, your own stunning patterns.

A good pattern flows smoothly, repeats in a satisfying rhythm, and balances color and texture. But what makes it truly special is the story or emotion it carries.

Step 1: Choosing Your Color Palette

Every great bracelet begins with color. Color isn't just decoration — it's expression. The shades you choose set the mood and energy of your design.

Here's how to experiment creatively:

Start with an emotion or theme.

Do you want your bracelet to feel calm and soothing? Try blues, greens, and whites.

Looking for energy and excitement? Go for reds, oranges, and yellows.

Want something mystical or elegant? Choose purples, silvers, or blacks.

Use gradients.

Blend from dark to light shades of the same color family — for example, deep turquoise to sky blue — to create a beautiful ombré effect.

Contrast boldly.

Combine complementary colors like pink and green, or blue and orange, for a vibrant pop.

Tell a story through color.

Perhaps you're making a bracelet for someone's birthday — use their favorite colors. Or design one inspired by a season:

Spring: Pastel pinks and greens

Summer: Bright yellows and turquoise

Autumn: Burnt orange, gold, and brown

Winter: Icy blues and white

There's no wrong choice — only the one that feels right to you.

Step 2: Mixing Materials

Once you've chosen your colors, consider mixing materials to give your design texture and sparkle. Experimenting with different fibers opens up a new world of creative expression.

Try these combinations:

Embroidery floss + metallic cord → Adds shimmer and luxury.

Hemp twine + cotton thread → Earthy and rustic, perfect for boho styles.

Nylon thread + beads → Sleek and modern.

Variegated thread (thread that changes color) → Creates automatic color transitions without extra planning.

You can also use thicker or thinner threads strategically. Mixing sizes adds dimension — thicker threads make bold lines, while thinner ones create subtle details.

The key is balance: experiment until the materials complement rather than compete.

Step 3: Designing Your Pattern Layout

Now comes the fun part — sketching your own design.

You don't need to be an artist or graphic designer; all you need is curiosity and patience.

Option 1: Graph Paper

Draw a series of small diamonds (each diamond represents a knot).

Assign colors to your threads at the top of the page.

Use arrows inside each diamond to show knot direction:

→ for forward knots

← for backward knots

↔ for forward-backward

⇄ for backward-forward

Start with a simple repeating pattern, like alternating diagonal stripes, then modify it by shifting colors or reversing directions.

Option 2: Online Pattern Generators

There are free online tools where you can create digital bracelet patterns. These allow you to select thread colors, directions, and repeat sections easily. Once your design is ready, you can print or save it for reference.

These tools are especially handy if you want to share your patterns online or recreate them later.

Step 4: Adding Symbols, Letters, or Shapes

Once you're comfortable designing geometric patterns, you can take your artistry further by creating pictures and symbols in your bracelets.

This technique is often called alpha pattern design, and it allows you to include shapes, hearts, stars, initials, or even words woven into your bracelet.

Here's how to start:

Think of your bracelet as a pixel grid — each knot represents one "pixel."

Sketch your design on graph paper, coloring in squares where you want your symbol or letter to appear.

Translate that sketch into knots. Each row becomes one line of your bracelet.

You can design monograms for friends, zodiac signs, small icons (like a sun, moon, or wave), or short words like "LOVE" or "PEACE."

This style requires a little more focus, but the results are incredibly rewarding — a bracelet that tells a story in symbols and color.

Step 5: Testing and Refining Your Design

Even the most beautiful design may look different when knotted. Threads behave in three dimensions, and colors may blend or contrast in unexpected ways. That's why testing is essential.

Make a small sample strip before committing to a full bracelet. This will show you how your pattern looks in real thread and help you adjust spacing, tension, or color order.

Ask yourself:

Do the colors blend the way I imagined?

Are the shapes clear and balanced?

Is the pattern too tight or too loose?

If something feels off, don't worry — adjusting is part of the creative process. You can change thread order, tweak knot directions, or simplify the design. With practice, your intuition will sharpen, and you'll start designing naturally, almost like sketching freehand.

Step 6: Naming and Recording Your Patterns

Every creation deserves a name! Naming your patterns not only helps you remember them but also celebrates your creative identity.

You can keep a pattern journal — a small notebook or digital file — where you:

Draw your patterns or print them out.

Record thread colors, materials, and notes about the process.

Include photos of the finished bracelet.

This is especially useful if you plan to sell or gift your creations, as it allows you to remake or modify designs easily.

Step 7: Finding Inspiration

Design inspiration can come from anywhere — nature, art, culture, or emotion.

Here are a few sources to spark your creativity:

Nature: Waves, flowers, leaves, or animal patterns.

Architecture: Geometric shapes, tiles, or stained glass windows.

Textiles: Traditional fabrics, indigenous patterns, or weaves from different cultures.

Music and Emotion: Try creating a "song bracelet" inspired by how a melody feels, or a "mood bracelet" reflecting your current emotion.

Sometimes, the best designs are spontaneous — start knotting and let your hands guide you.

Step 8: Embrace Your Signature Style

As you experiment, you'll notice that certain colors, materials, or motifs feel like "you." Maybe you love gradients that fade softly, or bold graphic shapes, or elegant minimalism. That's your signature style — your creative fingerprint.

Don't rush to define it; let it evolve naturally. The more bracelets you design, the more your personal aesthetic will emerge.

Remember, there's no "perfect" pattern — only authentic expression. Every knot you tie, every color you choose, tells a story that no one else can tell exactly the same way.

Final Reflection: Every Bracelet Tells Your Story

Designing your own patterns isn't just about decoration — it's about storytelling. Each bracelet becomes a reflection of your experiences, moods, and memories. The colors you choose might capture a feeling; the pattern you create might commemorate a friendship or a season in your life.

So, let your imagination guide you. Mix unexpected colors. Try new materials. Break traditional rules if you want to. Creativity flourishes when you give yourself permission to play.

Whether you're designing your first custom pattern or your hundredth, remember this simple truth:

Your bracelet doesn't have to be perfect — it just has to be yours.

Every knot you make, every thread you choose, carries your energy and intention. That's what makes it beautiful.

So, take your tools, clear a small space, and begin. There are endless patterns waiting to be discovered — all within your hands.